# 50 AND HOLDING YOUR OWN

## by
## JOHN PICKERING

## C C C   P U B L I C A T I O N S

Published by

CCC Publications
1111 Rancho Conejo Blvd.
Suites 411 & 412
Newbury Park, CA 91320

Published by arrangement with Powerfresh Limited of Northampton,
England.

U.S. version manufactured in the United States of America

ISBN: 0-918259-85-1

If your local U.S. bookstore is out of stock, copies of this book may be
obtained by mailing check or money order for $5.95 per book (plus
$2.50 to cover postage and handling ) to: CCC Publications; 1111
Rancho Conejo Blve.; Suites 411 & 412; Newbury Park, CA 91320

Pre-publication Edition - 4/96
First Printing - 7/96

# DON'T

HAPPY BIRTHDAY TO YOU,
HAPPY BIRTHDAY TO YOU,
HAPPY BIRTHDAY
**FIFTY PHOBIA**,
HAPPY BIRTHDAY TO YOU!

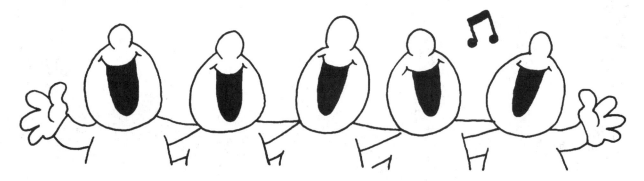

# BEING 50 CAN BE A TIME OF DISCOVERY...

ON HIS 50TH BIRTHDAY BOB DISCOVERED THAT HE WAS NO LONGER WORRIED ABOUT BEING 50 YEARS OLD — HE WAS NOW WORRIED ABOUT BEING 50 MILLION LIGHT YEARS FROM MIAMI!

ALICE WAS
HORRIFIED TO
DISCOVER THAT
SHE COULDN'T
SEE HER NAVEL
ANYMORE !

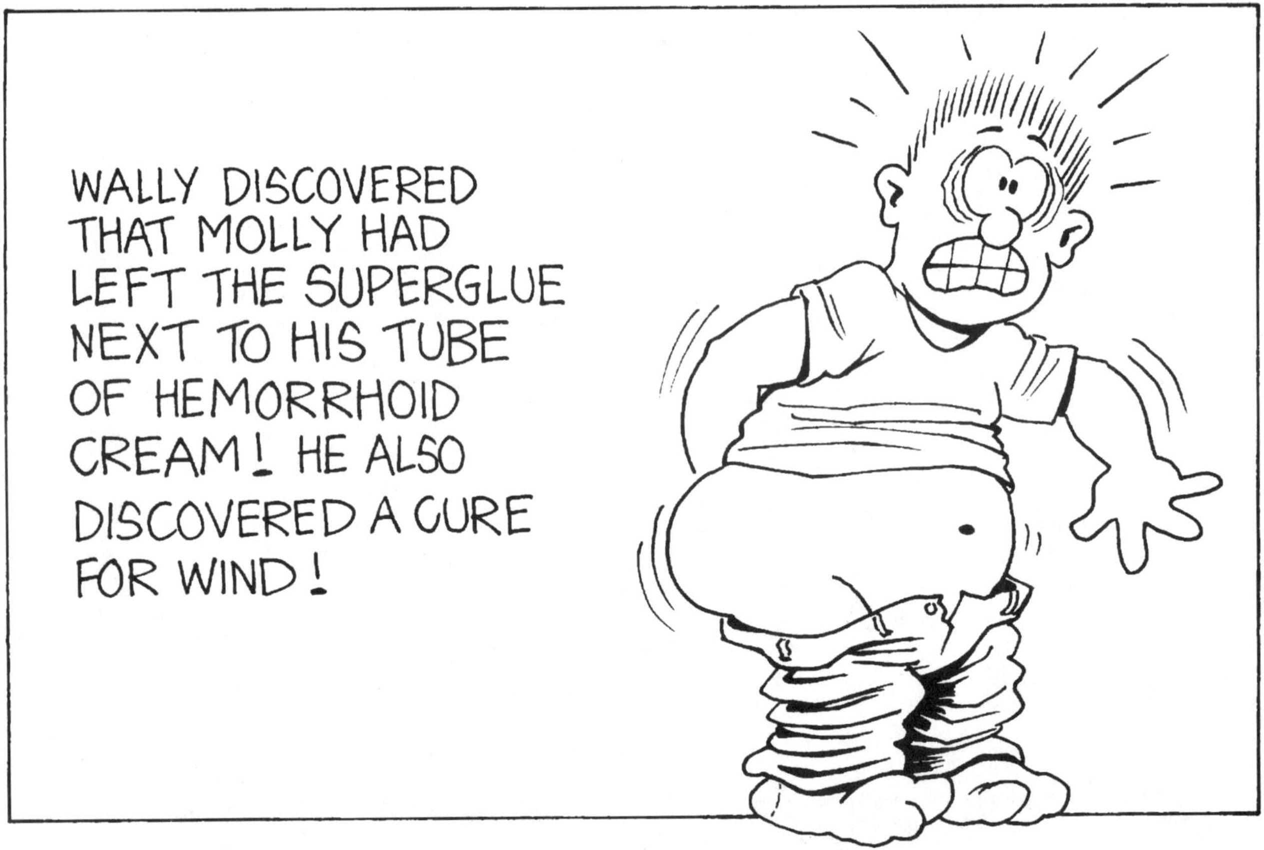
WALLY DISCOVERED THAT MOLLY HAD LEFT THE SUPERGLUE NEXT TO HIS TUBE OF HEMORRHOID CREAM! HE ALSO DISCOVERED A CURE FOR WIND!

ON HER 50TH BIRTHDAY MARY DISCOVERED THAT EVEN THOUGH SHE COULD STILL GET INTO A PAIR OF SIZE 10 LEVI'S, SHE WOULD PROBABLY HAVE TO HAVE THEM SURGICALLY REMOVED!

# THE 50 PLUS SURVIVAL KIT—FOR HIM!

CHECK THIS LIST TO SEE IF YOU HAVE GOT EVERYTHING YOU NEED!

1 HAIR DYE AND/OR TOUPEE
2 LOW FAT FOODS AND VITAMIN PILLS
3 FITNESS VIDEO (TO WATCH ONLY)
4 NEW SPORTY CAR WITH LOUD STEREO
5 LATEST 'TOP 40' CD'S
6 YOUNG BLOND BIMBO - 38-24-36
7 SEX GUIDE VIDEO (TO WATCH ONLY)
8 MEMBERSHIP OF NIGHT CLUB (DON'T DANCE!)
9 REGULAR VISITS TO PSYCHOTHERAPIST
10 SYMPATHETIC BANK MANAGER

# THE 50 PLUS SURVIVAL KIT – FOR HER!

1. HAIR COLOR AND VARIOUS WIGS
2. DIET AND SLIMMING MAGAZINES
3. EXERCISE VIDEO (WATCH ONLY)
4. NEW SEXY UNDERWEAR
5. AEROBICS CLUB MEMBERSHIP (DON'T GO)
6. REGULAR MASSAGE AND SUNBED SESSIONS
7. TOYBOY – 6 FT. TALL BODYBUILDER
8. COSMETIC SURGERY AND LIPOSUCTION
9. JOIN A WOMEN'S STUDIES GROUP
10. SECRET SUPPLY OF CHOCOLATES

WHEN THE PARACHUTE CLUB GAVE JONATHAN A SPECIAL BIRTHDAY JUMP
THEY FORGOT TO GIVE HIM A SPECIAL BIRTHDAY PARACHUTE!

SUE HAD CAREFULLY KEPT HER REAL AGE SECRET FROM EVERYONE,
EXCEPT HER IMMEDIATE FAMILY!

GEORGE HAD NOT EXPECTED THE GUYS TO HIRE A STRIPOGRAM GIRL AND NONE OF THEM HAD EXPECTED HER TO GO SO FAR!

TONY'S WORKMATES HAD ONE FINAL BIRTHDAY SURPRISE
FOR HIM —THEY HAD HIRED A CONTRACT KILLER !

WHEN LISA CAME OUT OF THE BATHROOM
SHE FOUND THAT DAVE HAD INVITED ALL THEIR FRIENDS IN FOR
HER SURPRISE BIRTHDAY PARTY!

EVERYONE LOVED
THE LOCAL NEWSPAPERS
50TH BIRTHDAY
PHOTOGRAPH OF THEIR
TOWN COUNCIL TREASURER,
GERALD VANDERBILT
AS A NUDE 4 YEAR OLD
SITTING ON HIS POTTY!

SECRETLY, GERALD
WONDERED IF HE
SHOULD SHOOT
OR POISON
HIS MOTHER!

HA, HA, HA!
HE, HE, HE!
HA, HA, HA!

The HERALD

WHEN PHIL REGAINED CONSCIOUSNESS HE WOULD LEARN WHY IT HAD NOT BEEN A GOOD IDEA TO BUY JILL THE 'FACELIFT AND LIPOSUCTION TREATMENT PACKAGE' AT THE COSMETIC SURGERY CLINIC FOR HER 50TH BIRTHDAY!

ON HIS 50TH BIRTHDAY ERIC WENT BACK TO VISIT THE LITTLE MEADOW WHERE LAY THE OLD 'LIGHTENING TREE' THAT HE HAD PLAYED ON AS A BOY. UNFORTUNATELY THIS WAS NOT ERIC'S LUCKY DAY!

# SOME POSITIVE 'FUN' THINGS TO DO TO OVERCOME THE FEAR OF BEING 50!

IF POSSIBLE THESE SHOULD BE DONE THE DAY **BEFORE** YOUR BIRTHDAY, WHILE YOU ARE STILL SANE ENOUGH TO THINK STRAIGHT!

FOR EXAMPLE:

JIM DECIDED TO CURE HIS SINUSITIS BY DRILLING OUT HIS NASAL CAVITIES WITH HIS POWER DRILL!

HELEN DECIDED
IT WAS TIME TO
FEEL GOOD ABOUT
HERSELF, SO SHE
TURNED THE
MAGNIFYING SIDE
OF HER MAKE-UP
MIRROR TO
THE WALL !

GORDON LOST HIS FEAR OF BEING 50 IN A NEW
FOUND VOCATION FOR FULL-TIME PRISON WORK !

CAROL SHOWED TOTAL DISREGARD FOR HER
50TH BIRTHDAY BY BUNGEE-JUMPING INTO A LIVE VOLCANO!

MARK DECIDED THAT DRIVING TO THE BAHAMAS
WOULD BE A GOOD WAY TO TAKE HIS MIND OFF HIS 50th BIRTHDAY!

EVERYONE SOON FORGOT ABOUT LINDA'S 50TH BIRTHDAY WHEN THEY SAW HOW WELL SHE COULD TIGHT-ROPE WALK IN THE NUDE!

JOHN SOON FORGOT ABOUT BEING 50 BY TAKING AN EXCITING TRIP TO A DISTANT PLACE WHERE NO ONE CARED HOW OLD HE WAS !

PAULA LOOKED EVERYWHERE
BUT SHE STILL COULDN'T FIND HER 'G' SPOT !

BELINDA DECIDED THAT SHE WOULD SPICE UP THEIR SEX LIFE
BUT MORRIS WAS TOO SCARED TO COME OUT FROM UNDER THE BED!

AS THE BED MOVED ACROSS THE ROOM MAVIS COULDN'T HELP WONDERING IF SHE SHOULD DEFROST THE TURKEY OR THE VEGETARIAN LASAGNE FOR DINNER TOMORROW!

FRANK HAD BEEN TOO EMBARRASSED TO BUY A PACK OF CONDOMS, SO HE'D BOUGHT A PACK OF BUBBLE GUM INSTEAD. RITA WAS NOT IMPRESSED!

MICK AND JEAN WERE RE-DISCOVERING THE JOY OF SEX.
BY 'POSITION 7' THEY DISCOVERED THAT THEY BOTH HAD SLIPPED DISCS!

WHEN THE GIRLS GAVE KAREN A CHROME-PLATED VIBRATOR FOR HER 50TH BIRTHDAY SHE THOUGHT IT WAS SOME KIND OF EXECUTIVE TOY. THEN SHE DISCOVERED ITS **REAL** FUNCTION... AN ELECTRIC ROLLING-PIN !

SOMETHING TOLD VICTOR THAT PAM DIDN'T WANT TO READ TONIGHT!

SINCE JOINING THE WOMEN'S ASSERTIVENESS GROUP FAY SEEMED
TO HAVE PROBLEMS DISTINGUISHING SEX FROM UN-ARMED COMBAT!

PAUL AND JUNE HAD BOUGHT A 'BETTER SEX' VIDEO, BUT BY THE TIME THE SEX THERAPIST HAD FINISHED TALKING THEY WERE BOTH FAST ASLEEP!

# THAT FIFTY FEELING

MATTHEW
TACTFULLY REFRAINED
FROM MENTIONING
THAT HIS DAD WAS NOT
ONLY **NOT** SCORING
ANY POINTS...
HE WAS ALSO
PLAYING 'MEGASONIC
UPSIDE DOWN !

SYLVIA HAD BEEN DETERMINED THAT BEING 50 WOULD NOT STOP HER PROVING TO HER DAUGHTER THAT SHE COULD ROLLER-DISCO AS WELL AS ANY 18 YEAR OLD!

KEVIN TRIED HARD TO DISGUISE THE FACT THAT HE WAS GOING BALD, BUT NO ONE WAS FOOLED!

BRENDA HAD
SPENT MANY SLEEPLESS
NIGHTS WORRYING
ABOUT HER WRINKLES
THEN ONE DAY
SHE WOKE UP WITH
CROWS FEET AND
HAD SOMETHING ELSE
TO WORRY ABOUT !

BURT HAD ALWAYS
BEEN A FAN OF
HORROR FILMS, BUT
WHEN HE WOKE UP ON
HIS 50TH BIRTHDAY
HE SUDDENLY REALIZED
THAT NOW HE WAS IN
THE TWILIGHT ZONE
FOR REAL !

WHEN ANDREW CAME HOME TO FIND HIS SON WATCHING A 'DIRTY' VIDEO OF SEXY NUDE LADIES DOING SEXY RUDE THINGS HE WAS ABSOLUTELY FURIOUS! WHY DIDN'T THEY HAVE VIDEOS LIKE THAT WHEN HE WAS A TEENAGER!

HARRY LIVED TO REGRET NOT HAVING A HAIR TRANSPLANT!

JENNY AND JOAN HAD BEEN IN THE SAME SIXTH-GRADE, BUT, STRANGELY, ALTHOUGH JENNY WAS NOW 50 JOAN WAS ONLY 44! CASUALLY JENNY PASSED HER COPY OF THEIR SIXTH-GRADE GROUP PHOTOGRAPH TO JOAN'S NEW BOY-FRIEND!

NOW HE WAS SO
GILBERT NOTICED
A STRANGE
PHENOMENON...
WHEN HE TOOK HIS
BELT OFF, HIS
TROUSERS DIDN'T
FALL DOWN !

TIME HAD JUST FLOWN SINCE DOROTHY WAS A 5 YEAR OLD. PLAYING IN THE MUD ON HER GRANDFATHER'S FARM—NOW SHE WAS A 50 YEAR OLD COVERED IN MUD IN A HEALTH FARM. DOROTHY WONDERED IF ALL THIS HAD SOME PROFOUND SPIRITUAL SIGNIFICANCE BUT MOSTLY SHE WONDERED IF THEY'D REMOVED ALL THE WORMS!

RAY HAD REALLY
BELIEVED 'YOU ARE ONLY
AS OLD AS THE WOMAN
YOU FEEL'...
THAT IS, UNTIL
SHE HAD TO HELP
HIM OFF THE DANCE
FLOOR AND CALL
THE PARAMEDICS !

WHEN VAL ASKED, "IF THE PIXELS TOOK SO MANY BITES WHAT WOULD THE ELVES EAT?" IT BECAME OBVIOUS TO EVERYONE ON THE COMPUTING COURSE THAT HER I.Q. WAS PROBABLY THE SAME AS HER AGE — ABOUT 50!

UNLIKE MANY MEN
HIS AGE, RALPH WAS
FIT ENOUGH TO TOUCH
THE FLOOR WITH
THE PALMS OF HIS HANDS.
UNFORTUNATELY HE
WAS NOT FIT ENOUGH
TO STRAIGHTEN
UP AGAIN!

ROGER KNEW HE WAS OVER THE HILL,
WHEN HE SUCKED HIS GUT IN...

...AND IT STILL HUNG OUT!

YOU KNOW YOU ARE PAST 50 WHEN...
SIGH!
YOU PREFER TO GO TO BED WITH A HOT WATER BOTTLE THAN WITH A HOT WOMAN!

JANICE JUST HAD TO FACE IT— SHE WAS NOW A 'GOLDEN OLDIE'...
ALL HER FAVORITE ARTISTS WERE IN THE EASY LISTENING SECTION!

YOU KNOW YOU ARE PAST 50 WHEN...

SOMEONE BUYS
YOU A T-SHIRT
FOR YOUR
50TH BIRTHDAY
AND YOU'RE NOT
SURE IF IT'S A
JOKE OR A
DEFINITION !

SAMANTHA KNEW THAT SHE WAS ON THE VERGE OF IMPENDING SENILITY WHEN SHE SAT UP TILL 2 IN THE MORNING AND **STILL** COULD NOT UNDERSTAND THE QUESTIONS IN HER 12 YEAR OLD SON'S MATH HOMEWORK!

YOU KNOW YOU ARE PAST 50 WHEN...
YOU ACTUALLY LOOK AS ROUGH AS YOUR OLD TEDDY!

AND FINALLY... WHEN EVERYONE HAS RE-INFORCED THE AWFUL FACT OF BEING **50**, THERE IS ONLY ONE THING YOU CAN SAY...

# TITLES BY CCC PUBLICATIONS

**Retail $4.99**

"?" book

POSITIVELY PREGNANT

WHY MEN ARE CLUELESS

CAN SEX IMPROVE YOUR GOLF?

THE COMPLETE BOOGER BOOK

FLYING FUNNIES

MARITAL BLISS & OXYMORONS

THE VERY VERY SEXY ADULT DOT-TO-DOT BOOK

THE DEFINITIVE FART BOOK

THE COMPLETE WIMP'S GUIDE TO SEX

THE CAT OWNER'S SHAPE UP MANUAL

PMS CRAZED: TOUCH ME AND I'LL KILL YOU!

RETIRED: LET THE GAMES BEGIN

THE OFFICE FROM HELL

FOOD & SEX

FITNESS FANATICS

YOUNGER MEN ARE BETTER THAN RETIN-A

BUT OSSIFER, IT'S NOT MY FAULT

**Retail $4.95**

YOU KNOW  YOU'RE AN OLD FART WHEN...

1001 WAYS TO PROCRASTINATE

HORMONES FROM HELL II

SHARING THE ROAD WITH IDIOTS

THE GREATEST ANSWERING MACHINE MESSAGES
OF ALL TIME

WHAT DO WE DO NOW?? (A Guide For New Parents)

HOW TO TALK YOU WAY OUT OF A TRAFFIC TICKET

THE BOTTOM HALF (How To Spot Incompetent
Professionals)

LIFE'S MOST EMBARRASSING MOMENTS

HOW TO ENTERTAIN PEOPLE YOU HATE

YOUR GUIDE TO CORPORATE SURVIVAL

THE SUPERIOR PERSON'S GUIDE TO EVERYDAY
IRRITATIONS

GIFTING RIGHT

**Retail $5.95**

LOVE DAT CAT
CRINKLED 'N' WRINKLED
SIGNS YOU'RE A GOLF ADDICT
SMART COMEBACKS FOR STUPID QUESTIONS
YIKES! IT'S ANOTHER BIRTHDAY
SEX IS A GAME
SEX AND YOUR STARS
SIGNS YOUR SEX LIFE IS DEAD
40 AND HOLDING YOUR OWN
50 AND HOLDING YOUR OWN
MALE BASHING: WOMEN'S FAVORITE PASTIME
THINGS YOU CAN DO WITH A USELESS MAN
MORE THINGS YOU CAN DO WITH A USELESS MAN
THE WORLD'S GREATEST PUT-DOWN LINES
LITTLE INSTRUCTION BOOK OF THE RICH & FAMOUS
WELCOME TO YOUR MIDLIFE CRISIS
GETTING EVEN WITH THE ANSWERING MACHINE
ARE YOU A SPORTS NUT?
MEN ARE PIGS / WOMEN ARE BITCHES

ARE WE DYSFUNCTIONAL YET?
TECHNOLOGY BYTES!
50 WAYS TO HUSTLE YOUR FRIENDS ($5.99)
HORMONES FROM HELL
HUSBANDS FROM HELL
KILLER BRAS & Other Hazards Of The 50's
IT'S BETTER TO BE OVER THE HILL THAN UNDER IT
HOW TO REALLY PARTY!!!
WORK SUCKS!
THE PEOPLE WATCHER'S FIELD GUIDE
THE UNOFFICIAL WOMEN'S DIVORCE GUIDE
THE ABSOLUTE LAST CHANCE DIET BOOK
FOR MEN ONLY (How To Survive Marriage)
THE UGLY TRUTH ABOUT MEN
NEVER A DULL CARD
RED HOT MONOGAMY
    (In Just 60 Seconds A Day) ($6.95)
HOW TO SURVIVE A JEWISH MOTHER ($6.95)
WHY MEN DON'T HAVE A CLUE ($7.99)
LADIES, START YOUR ENGINES! ($7.99)